HELP YOUR CHILD MANAGE THEIR MOODS

HELP YOUR CHILD MANAGE THEIR MOODS

An Hachette UK Company
www.hachette.co.uk

Vie Books, an imprint of Summersdale Publishers Ltd
Part of Octopus Publishing Group Limited
Carmelite House
50 Victoria Embankment
LONDON
EC4Y 0DZ
UK

www.summersdale.com

Printed and bound in Poland

ISBN: 978-1-78783-674-7

Substantial discounts on bulk quantities of Summersdale books are available to corporations, professional associations and other organizations. For details contact general enquiries: telephone: +44 (0) 1243 771107 or email: enquiries@summersdale.com.

HELP YOUR CHILD MANAGE THEIR MOODS

101 Ways to Cope With Big Feelings, Including Anger

LOUISE BATY

Disclaimer

CONTENTS

How to Use This Book

If you're reading this book, you may have concerns about your child's mood changes. It can be difficult, as a parent or carer, to watch your usually sunny child's mood darken, even temporarily.

Firstly, bear in mind that mood swings are standard during certain stages between five and 16. Sometimes these can be attributed to hormones or developmental changes. To complicate matters, kids usually aren't equipped with the language or maturity to express or deal with the feelings they're experiencing.

Also worth bearing in mind is the fact that, regardless of age, most of us experience anger occasionally. In fact, anger can be helpful – especially to a child – because it may indicate when a situation feels wrong or unfair. However, it can be hard to handle if your child experiences frequent bouts of "red mist" or if they're being aggressive and putting themselves or others at risk.

This book offers ways to help you understand and manage your child's mood changes with a holistic approach. It suggests various methods and strategies for identifying your child's anger triggers and ways in which you can help them manage their moods.

Do remember that each child is different, and when it comes to mood changes, there is no one-size-fits-all approach to tackling them. For that reason, don't aim to follow each point in this book rigidly. Instead, pick and choose the tips that appeal to you and which you feel may have a positive effect on your child.

Introduction

First, bear in mind that every child is unique, and different age groups and personality types may react differently to mood changes. Some children react physically; others "lash out" with words. Parents of older kids and teenagers could well be familiar with the slamming of doors after an argument.

You may recognize in your child some of the following common symptoms of anger, as outlined by the NHS, or they may tell you that they're experiencing them:

- **Clenched fists**
- **Racing heartbeat and tight chest**
- **Tense muscles**
- **Feeling hot**
- **Feeling nervous, tense or unable to relax**
- **Being easily irritated**
- **Feeling humiliated**
- **Feeling resentful of other people**
- **Shouting**
- **Sulking**
- **Breaking objects**
- **Starting fights**
- **Self-harming**

Try to remember that anger is a common human emotion. Read the tips in this book to help you and your child identify their anger triggers and experiment with methods for managing their moods. Hopefully you can gradually guide them to navigate life feeling calmer and happier.

CHAPTER 1

Talking and Listening

It may be difficult to coax your child into talking about their moods. They might not yet be able to make sense of their feelings or have the words to articulate them. They may also feel guilt or shame over their behaviour. This chapter outlines the gentlest ways to open up a conversation with your child.

Finding the right time and place to talk

You may be feeling worried about your child but be wary about rushing in too quickly to "sort things out". Instead, take your time and try to pick the best moment to talk to them about their feelings.

Remember that your child may be feeling as confused as you are. So be patient, and no matter how keen you are to talk to them about their feelings, don't announce a sit-down chat as this may be perceived as too formal and intimidating.

It's also a good idea to avoid trying to tackle things if your child is in the midst of an angry outburst. Waiting until they're feeling calmer is wise.

Kids tend to open up when you least expect it – on car journeys, for instance, when there are fewer distractions and there is no need for potentially awkward eye contact. Mealtimes can also be a good opportunity for a chat.

Alternatively, spend time with your child doing something they enjoy, such as colouring or playing a game. Once they're feeling relaxed and the conversation is already flowing, you might feel able to broach tricky subjects.

How to listen

As a parent, it's important to really listen to your child, so try to give them your full attention.

When your child starts to open up to you, put down your phone, turn off the TV, stop doing chores or whatever it is you're doing.

Make eye contact with them and demonstrate that you're really listening by offering a "reflection statement" – a psychologist technique.

Reflective listening* involves repeating what your child has said to you ("It makes me mad when you say that my room is too messy!") without twisting it or adding a different tone. So your reflection statement here could be "It makes you mad when I say your room is too messy but the reason I'd like you to tidy up is…" This makes your child feel heard and ensures that you've understood them correctly.

Empathize with their worries and don't downplay them. By belittling their concerns, you belittle your child, too.

*This term stems from work carried out by psychologist Carl Rogers

WHAT IS NORMAL FOR YOUR CHILD?

Remember that no one knows your child better than you do. That means there's no one better placed to judge whether your child's moods are "normal" for them or not.

Take time to assess their general moods and what is standard for them. This will help you to learn more about particular common triggers, such as hunger, tiredness or overstimulation. For instance, your child might usually be placid except at bedtime, indicating that tiredness is the cause of their angry outbursts.

If you can't apply the usual causes to your child's current emotional flare-ups – or if their mood swings seem more frequent – it may be time to look deeper.

Consider your child's age and stage

When looking at the bigger picture of your child's moods, bear in mind their age.

You may have left toddler tantrums behind but mood swings are characteristic of other developmental stages, such as pre-teens and teens. The average age for girls to start puberty is 11 and for boys it's 12. However, it can begin at any point between eight and 13 in girls and nine and 14 in boys.

Mood swings are a common part of puberty, due to surging hormones. Your child may be dealing with new, intense emotions, such as feeling angry or upset without understanding why.

Help your child know they are safe

As a parent or carer, our job is to make our child feel safe and secure enough to be able to grow and flourish. To do this, they need routine and structure at home: a calm, loving and fun environment without regular conflict, excessive shouting or physical punishment.

If their home life feels safe, the outside world won't seem so scary to them.

They need to know that their caregivers have "got their back" – so tell them that you love them, listen to them when they talk and give them a cuddle when they need one. Children should also feel the freedom to express themselves safely at home without fear of being questioned or ridiculed.

WAYS TO BOND

Give your child the most precious gift – your time.

It's important to bond with your child as an individual, away from siblings, as it strengthens the trust between you as caregiver and your child. Plan something without any agenda other than enjoying your time together. Ask them to suggest an activity, whether it's a favourite pastime or something new you're braving together.

You could:

- **Try a new sport**
- **See a movie**
- **Visit a new cafe**
- **Start a craft project**
- **Go for a walk in a favourite place**

Carving out time to spend just with them will boost their self-confidence and sense of self-worth. Once the plan is set, stick to it – by following through on your promise, you're reinforcing the trust between you, which will help your child to feel safe and secure.

How to talk about anger

Anger can be a tricky concept for adults to grasp, let alone children. When you find the right time for a chat with your child about their feelings, it's important to use the right words for their age and developmental stage – ones that they will understand.

For instance, perhaps a younger child feels "butterflies" in their stomach when they start to feel angry, or suddenly feels hot?

Maybe your teenager starts to feel anxious or unsettled when they're on the verge of an outburst?

Ask them to describe the way they feel and see if they can identify certain triggers that cause their mood changes. They may well surprise you by how perceptive they are.

When your child won't talk — different ways to communicate

Don't be surprised if your child clams up when you broach the subject of their moods.

Let's face it, many of us find it hard to express our feelings. To take the pressure off, make it a fun exercise by grabbing some paper and asking them to draw or write down their feelings.

Coloured crayons are particularly helpful for younger children as they may be keen to "colour their moods" and nothing says "anger" more than a scrawl of bright red!

Older children may feel able to brainstorm some useful words and write them down for you, giving you a springboard for that all-important heart-to-heart.

CHAPTER 2

Understand What Triggers Your Child's Moods

When tackling your child's mood changes, it's important to establish the cause. Some common triggers include struggling at school, friendship problems or being bullied. By pinpointing what is bothering your child, you may find it easier to help and support them. This chapter outlines ways to gauge your child's emotions – such as making an anger thermometer together or writing a mood journal – and understand how anger might feel for them.

Spot the symptoms

Remember that every child is different and that yours will demonstrate the onset of a mood change in different ways to others. However, by learning to detect those signs in your child as they occur, you stand a better chance of heading off an angry outburst before it escalates.

Some common early warning signs, according to the NHS, include:

- **Getting hot**
- **Looking flustered or panicky**
- **Clenching fists**
- **Gritting teeth**
- **Being heavy-handed with toys or other objects**
- **Going very quiet or suddenly vocal**
- **Becoming argumentative or snappy**

Spot the effects

Take note of the way your child behaves during an emotional outburst. Do they get physical, by throwing things, scratching, hitting or biting? Perhaps they let rip with words instead, shouting and screaming at you, siblings, friends or whoever else finds themselves in the firing line.

Maybe they're prone to sulking, or perhaps they're a door slammer and prefer to make a dramatic exit when feeling overwhelmed with anger.

By learning how your child reacts to mood changes, you can predict how a situation may pan out — and can then choose how to deal with it effectively.

HOW ANGER FEELS FOR YOUR CHILD

Remember that anger isn't just about intense rage and fury. In fact, those "eye of the storm" feelings may pass fairly swiftly for your child.

Once they've come through their immediate anger, they may be left with a combination of other bewildering emotions, such as fear, disappointment or sadness.

To lose control – even momentarily – can be frightening for a child and they may feel sad, disappointed or even embarrassed by their outburst. They may also feel exhausted physically and emotionally.

If you can, once they're calm again, ask your child how they felt during their angry outburst – it may give you real insight into what they're experiencing, and how you can tackle it together.

Thoughts are not facts

Sometimes we become so invested in our inner thoughts – particularly anxious or negative ones – that we convince ourselves they're actually true. This can be the case in people of all ages, young and old, but particularly in children.

Your child may think: "I always get everything wrong" or "I'm worthless".

They may become so stuck on this negative idea that, to them, it becomes a solid and immovable fact, which understandably affects their mood.

If your child is struggling, teach them that thoughts are not facts but are instead mental events that pop up in the mind as a result of our current mood. If your child is having a bad day, they may feel more bothered by certain thoughts.

Try this mindfulness exercise designed to help separate our inner thoughts from reality:

- Ask your child to explain their negative thought, such as "no one likes me".

- Now ask them if it's true. Initially, they may answer "yes".

- Ask them to think again – is it really true that no one likes them or could they look at this idea in a different way? Perhaps they're having an issue with just one friend at the moment but that doesn't mean that no one likes them at all.

- Ask them to reframe the thought in a more positive way – such as remembering all the people who do like and value them – and think about how this makes them feel.

Encourage them not to bottle up their anxious or negative thoughts but instead share them with you or other trusted people.

What you can and can't control

Kids like being in the driving seat when it comes to making such decisions as what to wear or what to eat. But it's impossible and unhealthy for them to always get their own way, and anger can stem from feelings of powerlessness and frustration when they're being prevented from doing whatever they want.

Help them understand the situations they can't control – such as why they can't live on a diet of junk food, walk to a friend's house after a certain time or have new toys and gadgets on demand.

Likewise, teach your child that they can't control other people's behaviour. Neither can they prevent things going "wrong", such as beloved toys being accidentally broken, or paintings being "ruined" when splashed with too much paint. (See page 61 for advice on perfectionism.)

Help your child see that the only thing in life they can control is their own behaviour and their reaction to things.

ANXIETY AND DEPRESSION IN YOUNG PEOPLE

Recent studies have shown that one in eight young people aged five to 19 suffer from a mental health disorder, with 7.2 per cent of children having an anxiety disorder.*

Yet many children struggle to express their feelings and may display other symptoms, such as low confidence, lack of concentration, sleeping and eating difficulties, tearfulness, irritability, negative thoughts and angry outbursts.

Some children are naturally more anxious than others, but some may develop anxiety due to stressful events, such as bereavement, conflict at home or issues at school.

If you're concerned that a mental health issue is affecting your child, you could speak to a professional, such as your family doctor or a trusted teacher at school. The charities Mind and Anxiety UK also offer advice.

*Source: NHS

Phobias

If your child regularly becomes angry and distressed in specific circumstances and the issue has lasted longer than six months, then consider that they may have a phobia.

A phobia goes beyond "normal" fears. In some sufferers, thinking about the cause of their phobia can prompt mood changes.

Children and teenagers are more prone to specific phobias than more complex ones, such as:

- **Fear of a certain type of animal or insect**
- **Certain situations where they may feel out of control, such as flying or visiting the dentist**
- **Environmental phobias, such as heights or deep water**
- **Phobias relating to the body, such as seeing blood or having injections**

Not all phobias need treatment – such as gradual exposure to the cause of the fear – but if whatever is causing the anxiety is difficult to avoid or the phobia is hindering your child's ability to function on a day-to-day basis, it would be advisable to seek professional guidance from your doctor.

Keep a diary

Keeping a mood journal can be an effective way of tracking your child's moods. Jot down instances of mood changes and angry outbursts in a diary or a notebook. If you can, include the trigger and the way that your child reacted. It might help to include the time, place, situation and who was there.

By keeping a record of your child's mood changes, you can build a clearer picture of the situation and may notice a pattern to their behaviour. For instance, if mood changes are more apparent at the end of the school week, it may indicate that tiredness is a trigger. If your child is old enough and willing, suggest they keep their own mood diary to help them better track and understand their emotions.

CREATE AN ANGER THERMOMETER

You and your child may find it helpful to mark each occurrence of anger out of ten with an "anger thermometer" – a simple way for your child to articulate the severity of their moods and a popular tool employed in child therapy.

For instance, your child may become argumentative over something but consider that the situation only merits a three on the anger thermometer.

In contrast, a full-blown outburst may be marked as a nine.

By knowing how greatly your child's moods are affected by certain situations, you can work on dealing with them together. If your child likes props, draw or download a simple picture of a thermometer with numbers from one to ten so that they can point to the appropriate anger level. For very young children who are still learning numbers, you could use varying emojis – happy, sad, cross – as a way of rating their feelings.

Ways to cope when your child is angry

It can be hard to know what to do in the moment when your child is angry, but here are some simple dos and don'ts:

Do:

- **Remember that this is about them, not you, so don't take it to heart.**
- **Ensure that they're safe — remove any sharp or heavy items from their grasp or reach.**
- **If you're in public, try to ignore any onlookers — your child is your priority.**
- **Give consequences for their behaviour (such as throwing or hitting), not their feelings. Teach them that anger is a normal emotion and that you will help them learn how to deal with it.**

Don't:

- **Freeze or panic — stay calm.**
- **Raise your voice as this will only antagonize them further.**
- **Try to reason with them or ask them to explain why they're angry right then and there as that's only likely to make things worse.**
- **Get physical with your child, shoving or manhandling them.**

What to say while they are angry

When your child feels overwhelmed with emotion, it's your job to stay calm and guide them safely through it with soothing language and actions.

Use simple, positive statements to show them that you're on their side: "I can see you're angry and it's okay to let it out."

Be firm about what is and isn't acceptable: "I know you're cross but I won't let you hit me."

Reassure them that you're supporting them: "I'm here and I love you."

Explain what you're doing: "I'm going to wait until you've stopped shouting and then maybe we can talk."

Offer comfort but don't force it: "Do you think you might like a cuddle? I'm here if you do."

WHAT NOT TO SAY WHEN THEY'RE ANGRY

Don't shout back or tell them off for feeling angry.

Don't say "You're making me cross."

Don't dismiss or minimize their feelings by telling them to "calm down", "stop screaming" or "stop whining". Try saying: "I can't understand you when you're talking in that way – can you talk more calmly, please?"

Don't try to shame them by calling them "spoilt" or "naughty".

If you're in a public place, resist the urge to hiss, "You're embarrassing me!" Your child isn't having an outburst to show you up; they're overwhelmed with emotion. Try saying: "Shall we go and talk about this somewhere quieter and try to work it out as a team?"

Don't take it personally

It's hard not to feel hurt when you're bearing the brunt of your child's latest angry outburst. But try not to take it personally.

Your child isn't deliberately "playing up" to ruin your day. In fact, this really isn't about you and it doesn't mean that you're a bad parent.

But when your child has lost control of their emotions, they will look to you for calming reassurance. So if you find yourself asking, "Why are you doing this to me?" or losing control of your own emotions in response to their behaviour, it may be time to step back briefly.

Providing your child is safe, it's fine to turn around momentarily or retreat to another room to gather your composure.

How to express emotions in a healthy way

Teach your child that it's okay — and perfectly normal — to experience strong emotions but that some ways of expressing them are healthier than others.

Be your child's role model by demonstrating how to handle strong emotions positively. Speak calmly rather than shouting or yelling around them.

Explain to them how you deal with your own feelings.

For example, you could say: "I felt really cross the other day when I lost my keys. But instead of shouting, I took a breath, counted to five and tried to remember where I'd left them. It really helped me feel better. Do you think it would help you too?"

HOW TO TACKLE ANGER TOGETHER

It's important that your child knows you're on their side when it comes to dealing with their emotions. To reinforce the idea that you're a team, work on nurturing the trust you share. You can do this by being there for them – to listen and to offer advice and encourage them to be open about their feelings with you so that you can work through them together.

Reassure them that you aren't upset or disappointed with them or their emotions and explain that what they're experiencing is completely normal. Tell them: "Everyone gets angry sometimes. What counts is how you deal with it."

Offer your child ways to express their anger. For instance, younger children may enjoy "drawing their anger" with you – maybe anger could be a fire-breathing dragon or an erupting volcano?

Older children might like to burn off steam with some exercise, such as going for a jog or kicking a ball around with you.

If you can, ask them if there's anything in particular they'd like you to do when they're feeling overwhelmed. For instance, would a hug help in the moment or would they prefer to be given some space?

Take a breath

Teach your child one of the simplest mindfulness techniques around – taking a deep breath.

When emotions threaten to overwhelm us, it can be really helpful to take a moment to breathe in deeply and exhale slowly.

This gives us time to gather our thoughts momentarily and, hopefully, stop anger in its tracks. Also, it's so easy and can be done by adults and children alike.

When you notice your child demonstrating the early warning signs of anger, try calmly telling them: "Take a deep breath and then let's talk about how you're feeling." Try it yourself and see the positive effects.

Count to ten

You may remember being told to count to ten as a child yourself because it's a technique that has been used for generations.

Now research* has found that, in certain situations, the count-to-ten method can help reduce aggression. Counting methodically is familiar and accessible to most children from the age of five. It's also a simple distraction method, a way of teaching your child to take a few moments when they sense their mood changing. By counting – either aloud or in their head – they give themselves time to calm down and allow their anger to subside.

*Source: *The Journal of Applied Social Psychology*, Jeffrey Osgood and Mark Muraven at the State University of New York.

CHAPTER 3

Help Your Child to Feel Calm

This chapter looks at ways to promote and instil calmness. When you find go-to methods that work for your child, such as yoga, painting or walking in nature, you can start to include them in their daily routine. Every child responds differently to soothing activities and mindfulness techniques so don't be afraid to experiment and see what works best.

40

Mind- and body-calming activities

There are many simple, soothing activities to try that could quickly calm your child. Have a think about what makes them relaxed and happy. It could be listening to a favourite song or baking cookies together. Here are some ideas:

- **Make them a cooling drink of water to avoid dehydration if they're crying, or a cosy beverage, such as hot chocolate — it's like a warm hug in a mug!**

- **Run your child a bath or shower so they can enjoy some "time out" in soothing water (under supervision if required).**

- **Do something creative, such as painting or playing with modelling clay.**

- **Build something imaginative with Lego.**

- **Listen to relaxing music.**

- **Do a jigsaw.**

- **Go for a walk in nature.**

- **Watch fish swimming in an aquarium or view online videos of fish swimming (research* has found that it can reduce blood pressure and heart rate).**

*Source: University of Exeter, UK

Mindfulness meditation

Learn about mindfulness meditation – an ancient practice described in Buddhist philosophy as "lucid awareness". Simply put, mindfulness is a way of separating yourself from external influences and peripheral worries and grounding yourself in the present moment.

It's so easy for children to follow, mindfulness techniques are now taught in schools worldwide.

There are many benefits to children practising mindfulness meditation:

- Promotes patience, a happier outlook and feelings of contentment
- Teaches simple ways to stay calm in stressful situations that they can carry with them to adulthood
- Boosts attentiveness
- Improves memory, cognitive control and flexibility, which can help with their studies and especially when taking exams

FIVE-SENSES MEDITATION

Try the "five senses" exercise as a way of getting your child to focus on their senses, not their thoughts.

- **Ask your child to notice five things they can see — get them to take a really good look at your environment. Is there anything unusual that they don't typically notice?**

- **Then ask them to notice four things they can feel — the texture of their clothing, for instance.**

- **Next, ask them to notice three things they can hear — encourage them to listen for background noises they usually filter out, such as birds chirping or a kettle boiling.**

- **Then ask them to notice two things they can smell — either pleasant or unpleasant!**

- **Lastly, ask them to notice one thing they can taste — give them a drink and suggest they sip it and savour the flavour.**

Grounding meditation

If someone is "ungrounded", they may struggle with how they channel their energy and display such signs as:

- **Being unable to think clearly**
- **Finding it hard to relax or sleep**
- **Feeling overwhelmed and tense**
- **Wanting to snack frequently**
- **Struggling to concentrate**
- **Reacting strongly to triggers, such as certain people or situations**

Stimulants including sugar and technology, along with limited physical outdoor activity, can cause kids to feel "ungrounded".

For an easy grounding exercise, ask your child to take off their shoes and socks and stand up straight, feeling their connection with the ground. Ask them to take deep breaths and imagine that they're a tree. Their feet are the firmly planted roots, their body is the strong tree trunk and their arms are branches.

Relaxation
techniques

Practise these three simple relaxation techniques with your child to reduce stress and frustration:

- Create homemade stress balls. First, fill balloons with rice or dry lentils then squeeze the ball in one or both hands. Try different speeds and a variety of pressures.

- Pretend to be a sleepy cat waking from a nap, easing and tensing your hands into fists. Exercise your facial muscles by meowing and yawning. Stretch out your legs and arms and arch your back like a cat.

- Try guided visualization. Ask your child to close their eyes and listen as you tell a story leading them to imagine themselves in a calm, relaxing place, such as a beach. As they focus on your story, their worries should melt away. Many simple guided visualization scripts are also available online.

COLOURING

A colouring book and a pot of pens can work wonders as a stress-reliever. In fact, some experts believe colouring to be as relaxing as meditation, because it encourages your brain to focus on this one activity in the moment, reducing anxiety and other negative emotions.

As colouring books have become a well-established mindfulness tool in recent years, you should be able to find one suitable for your child, whatever their age.

Bear in mind, too, that colouring can also be a wonderful shared bonding activity so why not offer to help out with their picture?

Reading

To open a book is to step into a magical new world, far away from the worries of everyday life. Research by The Reading Agency charity has found that reading can be a real mood-booster.

Not only does it increase a sense of empathy and encourage better relationships with others, it has also been found to reduce the symptoms of depression and improve overall well-being.

Encourage your child to pick up a book regularly, whether you read to them, they read aloud to you or they curl up on their own with a favourite story.

Age-appropriate audio books are also a wonderful, relaxing way to get lost in stories.

Exercise together

Exercise is ideal for letting off steam and a jog or cycle ride can be a quick way to quell anger when it starts to grow. It's a great idea to build regular exercise into your routine, so try to set aside 30 minutes three times a week for fun physical activities with your child. It not only benefits physical health but also has many positive effects on mental well-being, especially if you get out in nature for your exercise session.

You could incorporate exercise into your day by:

- Going for a brisk family walk
- Getting on your bikes and exploring new routes
- Setting up a home fitness circuit with such activities as jogging on the spot, hula-hooping and rope-skipping
- Kicking a ball around
- Putting on your favourite tunes and having a family disco
- Following a child-friendly online yoga video

BEING IN NATURE

If your child is happiest jumping in muddy puddles, try to nurture their love of the great outdoors by going out in all weathers and making it a regular ritual.

A study* found that two thirds of people instinctively retreat to a natural setting when they're stressed. Being in nature – or even just viewing nature scenes – helps to dispel anger. There are other benefits, too, such as reducing cortisol, boosting memory, lowering blood pressure, easing depression and anxiety, improving focus and boosting the immune system.

To encourage your little nature-lover, you could:

- **Take them to the woods, park or local nature reserve**
- **Challenge them to spot flowers and bugs outdoors**
- **Help them grow seedlings in a pot**

Most importantly, don't stress if they get thoroughly filthy – it's all part of the fun!

*Source: Marcus and Barnes

Spending time with animals

The companionship a pet offers not only eases anxiety, but it can also nurture a child's self-confidence as well as providing a sense of purpose, routine and responsibility.

Spending time with a pet also enables a child to live joyfully "in the moment" – so if you are lucky enough to have a pet, try to encourage your child to spend time with it and help care for it each day.

A study by Washington State University found that spending just ten minutes interacting with a dog or cat significantly reduces the stress hormone cortisol.

If you don't have a family pet, why not visit someone who does, or take your child to a petting farm or zoo so they can, under supervision, spend time with animals.

Breathing techniques

Focusing on breathing can be a great way to calm an anxious or angry child.

Try feather breathing:

- Rest a feather on the palm of your child's hand.
- Tell them to hold their hand just beneath their chin.
- Instruct them to breathe normally and watch how the feather moves as they inhale and exhale.

Taking slow, deep breaths can also be very effective.

Try balloon breathing:

- Ask your child to sit down and close their eyes.
- Tell them to imagine that their tummy is a balloon.
- Instruct them to "fill up the balloon" by breathing in for three counts.
- Tell them to "let out the air" by breathing out for three counts.
- Repeat several times.

DOODLING

Don't dismiss doodling as a mindless act of boredom. In fact, doodling has been found* to have many benefits, such as improving concentration, boosting memory, alleviating stress and helping the doodler to be more present in the moment. Children may find it relaxing and enjoyable to draw repeat patterns or swirls – whatever comes into their mind.

Some children may find doodling more soothing and less pressured than colouring because it's uncomplicated and the stakes are low – there is no "wrong" way to do it. Others will prefer the structure of colouring. Every child is different, after all.

Prompt your child to pick up a pencil or pen and draw shapes or patterns that come naturally. Encourage them just to let their pen flow over the paper without thinking about the end result and see what happens.

*Source: A study by psychologist Jackie Andrade of the University of Plymouth, UK

Make a den

Den-building can be magical and, if you offer to help out, you'll get the chance to bond with your child, with them as the leader of the exercise and with the pressure firmly off.

Whether your child opts to construct their den with cardboard boxes, a blanket slung over some chairs or twigs and branches outdoors, they'll relish having their special place – somewhere to play and relax in peace.

If you don't have space for a permanent den in your home, don't worry. It's a simple yet effective process that can easily be repeated whenever your child's emotions bubble over.

Singing

Singing aloud can calm your child and be a great mood-booster because it releases endorphins, the "happy hormone", giving an instant lift, easing anxiety and tension.

Whether your child's musical tastes involve nursery rhymes or pop, encourage them to turn up the volume and lose themselves in their favourite songs.

They may want to belt out a tune with you in the car, or they might prefer to retreat to their room for a solo sing-along. As with all mindfulness methods, there is no right or wrong way as long as it's boosting their mood.

HAVE A LAUGH

A sense of humour can carry us through life and, in fact, research* has found that laughing with others releases feel-good endorphins, too.

Learning to laugh at difficult situations and to not take ourselves too seriously is also an important life lesson.

Teach your kids a sense of humour by telling funny stories of your own, cracking jokes, reading laugh-out-loud books and singing humorous songs together. However, remind them that humour should never be mean-spirited or designed to upset others.

* Source: Studies by University of Oxford, UK, University of Turku, Finland and Aalto University, Finland

CHAPTER 4

Boost Your Child's Self-Esteem

This chapter examines ways to nurture and bolster your child's self-esteem so that they have the resilience and confidence to cope with and diffuse tricky emotions. Learn methods to help your child banish negativity with positive thoughts and gratitude, cultivate and cherish friendships, embrace family time and, above all, treat themselves with kindness.

Treat yourself kindly

Teach your child that self-compassion is equally as important as treating others with kindness. When we perceive things to be going wrong, many of us default to shaming ourselves with our own negative "inner voice" even though we'd never dream of judging others so harshly.

Ask your child to consider how they'd treat a friend who was lacking in confidence. Would they berate them or would they be kind and caring? Perhaps they'd say: "You shouldn't feel bad about yourself – you're a good person, who is loved, and has many skills and talents."

Now ask them to imagine that, instead of a friend, they're talking to themselves. Using the same reassuring tone of voice, they should repeat the statement, replacing "You" with "I".

Think positive

Listen to how your child speaks aloud to themselves when they're frustrated. If they say "I always mess up," there's a good chance they're plagued by negative thoughts. They may also turn their negativity on other people or certain situations.

Be your child's role model by avoiding moaning or speaking badly about yourself or others. Encourage positive thinking instead and looking on the bright side of tricky situations.

Try a modern take on counting your blessings by asking your child to say five positive things about their lives right now – one for each digit on one hand.

Teach them to replace negativity with positivity – rather than saying: "I always mess up," how about "I always try my best"?

SELF-ESTEEM

Low self-esteem can lead to difficulties including anger and depression. Here are some basic rules to live by that will help your child build a positive opinion of themselves from a young age:

- **When they need you, give them your undivided attention.**

- **Talk calmly to them.**

- **Praise them when merited.**

- **Don't demean or belittle them.**

- **Love them unconditionally and never make them feel ashamed for being themselves.**

- **Focus on their strengths and nurture their unique talents.**

- **Teach them that no one has more or less worth than them.**

- **Guide them to see mistakes as stepping stones for learning.**

- **Encourage and help them to learn life skills.**

Perfectionism

Some children can become angry and emotional over seemingly unimportant events, such as accidentally dripping paint over their latest artwork.

Perfectionism and low self-esteem are often linked because those with a poor opinion of themselves tend to focus on their perceived failures or inadequacies.

Learning to adapt to disappointment and not "sweat the small stuff" is something that can come with time and life experience. Reassure your child that, generally, things turn out all right, even if the outcome is not what you expected.

For instance, you could tell a younger child: "How about we make those paint blobs on your picture into funny faces?" To help an older child, who may be upset about not achieving top scores in a school test, you could explain that test results aren't everything in life — and that they have many skills and talents.

Help them accept and move on from setbacks and see them as learning opportunities. Most importantly, teach them that life in general isn't perfect.

Role-play scenarios

Try acting out situations in which your child might feel angry. It's a useful process for learning to express strong emotions in a healthy, positive way.

For instance, you could play the part of a friend who's refusing to let your child share the equipment at the park. Ask your child how they'd react and what they'd say. Then come up with some useful solutions for dealing with the issue calmly.

Another scenario could be that your child is watching a movie when they should be getting on with homework — and feels unfairly treated when you ask them to switch off the TV and do their work. Talk calmly about how you understand their frustration but explain the importance of doing the things they have to do (homework) before they can do the things they want to do (watch TV). Act out how you could both deal with this situation calmly — show your child that if they agree to turn off the TV without arguing, they will be allowed to finish watching their movie once they've completed their homework.

POSITIVE AFFIRMATIONS

Encourage your child to come up with positive affirmations – confidence-boosting statements about themselves, such as "I'm a great friend," "I'm good at sports" or "I have a talent for art."

Affirmations are a great way to build self-esteem. Here are some ideas for making them fun rather than a chore:

- **Hang a notice board in your kitchen or hallway and ask your child to pin positive affirmations there so they can read them every day.**

- **Create an affirmations treasure chest — make or buy a box and ask your child to write positive affirmations and store them in it. Refer to the treasure chest when needed.**

- **Turn your child's positive affirmations into songs you can sing together.**

Cultivating friendships

Encourage your child to make and maintain friendships. During childhood, friendships are important for development, and research* has even linked having a good-quality reciprocated friendship during school years with relationship quality in later years.

Friendships enrich our lives by boosting happiness, reducing stress, improving self-confidence and self-esteem, as well as helping us cope with difficult life events. They can also broaden our horizons and view of the world.

Try to nurture your child's social skills, such as:

- **Being able to strike up conversations — can your child think of ways to start social interactions; sometimes a simple "Hello. What's your name?" will suffice!**

- **Interpreting social situations — can your child "read" a social situation and know when to start and stop talking?**

- **Listening to others — a basic rule of conversation that involves your child focusing on what the other child is saying to them**

- **Interacting positively — being kind, polite and respectful of others**

*Source: Catherine Bagwell, professor of psychology at Oxford College, Emory University, USA

Spending time with friends

Recognize how important your child's friendships are to their well-being and aim to provide opportunities for them to see friends outside school.

Research* shows that a child's friendships have profound positive effects on their social and emotional development as well as their mental health and academic progress. What's more, your child doesn't have to be the most popular kid in class — they may only need one reciprocal friendship to make a difference.

Be a role model to your child by demonstrating healthy social interactions. Teach them to play nicely, share and cooperate with their peers.

*Source: Catherine Bagwell, professor of psychology at Oxford College, Emory University, USA

TRY SOMETHING NEW

Don't let your child get stuck in a rut by always doing the same things. Instead, encourage them to challenge themselves by stepping out of their comfort zone.

All too often, we let the fear of the unfamiliar hold us back but trying a new activity can be a real confidence booster, allowing us to press the "reset" button on our lives. So shake things up by persuading them to try a different sport or hobby or venturing to the park across town rather than going to the usual one closest to home. Remember that new ventures can also provide opportunities for meeting new friends.

And if, afterwards, your child decides that it's not for them, don't sweat it — at least they can say they've tried it!

Turning off gadgets

Spending extended periods looking at screens is associated with an unhealthy diet and lack of exercise.

Then there's the influence of social media; when your child is using their gadgets to look at other people's photos and videos, they're observing life – or rather a carefully curated highlights reel of someone else's life – rather than experiencing it first-hand.

Worryingly, multiple studies have found that heavy or excessive social media use can increase risk for depression, anxiety, loneliness, self-harm and even suicidal thoughts. Social media may also lead to feelings of inadequacy about your own life along with "fear of missing out" (FOMO).

Experts* recommend setting age-appropriate screen-time limits. It's also recommended that you switch off phones, laptops and tablets at least an hour before bedtime to avoid hindering sleep.

Don't forget your own device either. By powering off all screens, you and your child will have more opportunities to spend undistracted quality time together.

*Source: Royal College of Paediatrics and Child Health

Family time

It sounds simple because it is! Spend time with your child.

Families need quality time to bond and to develop strong, deep ties. By organizing regular opportunities to be with your child, you help them feel safe and protected. Sadly, kids who feel that their parents never make time for them may end up feeling rejected and angry.

You don't need expensive days out to make it count. Sparing an hour to go for a walk together can make all the difference. The important thing is that you spend that time focusing on your child, talking and listening to them.

KEEP A DAILY GRATITUDE JOURNAL

Every evening, ask your child to write down three good things from their day – big or small – in a notebook.

Practising gratitude regularly has been found to improve happiness and well-being.* You can prompt your child by starting off their sentences, such as "One fun thing I did today was…" or "A good thing that happened to me today was…"

If your child is reluctant to keep a journal, have a daily gratitude conversation instead. During dinner or at bedtime, tell each other your "three good things".

*Source: Studies undertaken at the University of California and the University of Miami, USA

Get a Vitamin D boost

Ensure your child is getting enough Vitamin D, which has been proven to help regulate mood and ease depression and anxiety.

Top up your child's intake with Vitamin D-rich foods including egg yolks, mushrooms and oily fish, such as salmon and mackerel. Vitamin D can be found in some fortified cereals, juices and milk, and you could also try a child-safe supplement.

Don't forget that getting outside in the sunshine is the ideal way to increase Vitamin D levels. Daily exposure of ten to 30 minutes can make a real difference.

CHAPTER 5

Create a Calming Home Environment

By living calmly yourself – ensuring you get enough sleep and exercise, taking time out for self-care and eating a balanced diet – you may find that your child is less inclined to mood swings. Try some of these tips for creating a home environment where your child feels safe and able to relax and manage their emotions more effectively.

Eating well

Provide your child with a balanced diet.

Eating well increases energy levels, boosts memory function and maintains a sense of well-being.

On the flipside, eating unhealthy food may leave your child lethargic and less equipped to cope with schoolwork.

As a guide, the World Health Organization (WHO) recommends that children:

- **Eat at least five portions of fruit and vegetables a day**
- **Include whole grains and nuts in their diet**
- **Shift fat consumption away from foods high in saturated fats, such as red meat, butter and cheese, to foods high in unsaturated fats, such as olives, peanut butter and avocados**
- **Limit sugar intake by reducing consumption of such sugary foods as chocolate, ice cream and sweets**

Try to serve balanced meals containing protein, whole grains and vegetables. Choose raw vegetables and fruit for snacks rather than crisps and biscuits. Avoid sugary, fizzy drinks.

Drink water

Encourage your child to stay hydrated. Research* has found that dehydration can quickly cause headaches, loss of focus and irritability. But when children are busy playing or studying, they may not notice feeling thirsty.

Buy younger children a spill-proof cup to keep close and encourage them to take regular sips.

The European Food Safety Authority (EFSA) recommends children between the ages of four and 13 should drink approximately six to eight glasses of fluid a day. On hotter days, or if they've been particularly active, they may require more.

*Source: *The Journal of Nutrition*

REGULAR EXERCISE

Experts recommend that children and teenagers should do at least an hour of physical activity daily. This could take the form of playing in the park, bouncing on a trampoline or organized exercise, such as swimming lessons or athletics club. Bear in mind that children tend to be active in short bursts rather than for long periods.

Physical activity keeps our minds as well as our bodies in shape by stimulating the production of endorphins, which boost well-being and improve sleep patterns. It also releases cortisol, which helps us manage stress.

Stretch

Along with improving your child's flexibility and posture, stretching exercises prompt them to focus on their bodies and breathing, which could boost their mood. Ensure that your child only stretches once their muscles are already warm from other exercise.

Yoga can be ideal for incorporating stretching into your child's routine. You'll find child-friendly yoga tutorials online or try the simple Child's Pose:

- **Kneel with your toes touching and your knees together or apart.**
- **Stretch your arms in front of your head with your hands palm-down on the floor or hold them by your side with your palms up.**
- **Gradually bend until your forehead is on the ground.**
- **Inhale and exhale slowly.**
- **Hold the pose for three to five breaths.**

Switch off for sleep

Turn off phones, tablets and laptops at least an hour before bedtime. The blue light emitted by these LED-based devices stimulates the stress hormone cortisol and interferes with the production of sleep-inducing melatonin, which we need to fall asleep.

Switch off the TV, too, especially if your child favours high-octane shows that get them hyped up. Brain-stimulating games and activities should also be paused until the next day. Instead, introduce bedtime reading, audio books or soothing music.

You could also offer a warm, milky drink at bedtime — milk and other dairy products contain an amino acid that helps induce sleep. As quinoa is high in amino acids, it's a great option for vegans. Try making quinoa milk at home by blending cooked quinoa with water and sweetening it with dates and cinnamon.

MAKE YOUR CHILD'S BEDROOM CONDUCIVE TO A GOOD NIGHT'S SLEEP

Follow these ideas for creating an optimal sleep environment for your child:

- **Use blackout blinds or curtains to avoid chinks of light coming into your child's bedroom and preventing them from relaxing.**

- **Turn off their bedroom's main lights because bright lights trick the body into "daytime" mode.**

- **Use a low-light reading lamp or night light.**

- **Organize an easy storage system so that you can clear away toys and clutter with minimal effort.**

- **Ensure their bed is comfy, with clean sheets, and that their favourite comforter or cuddly toy is easy to locate.**

- **Consider installing speakers for playing soothing bedtime music or audiobooks.**

- **Ensure the room isn't too hot or too cold — 16–18°C is thought to be the ideal temperature in a bedroom.**

Declutter

Not only does mess look unsightly, it can affect mental health. Research* has found that people living amid clutter suffer higher stress levels.

- **If your home is uncomfortably cluttered, lead by example and teach your child to let things go.**

- **Follow a "one-in, one-out" policy; only introduce a new item to replace something.**

- **Don't let unused items accumulate — when your child grows out of clothes or toys, pass them on.**

- **Photograph your child's paintings and crafts so that you have a digital memory rather than a physical one.**

- **If your child's room is messy, help them declutter so that they have less to tidy away each day.**

*Source: University of California, USA

Make your home a sanctuary

Think about how to make your home a peaceful, safe space for your child.

Don't strive for "show home" standards but keep rooms clean and uncluttered. Encourage slow living — home is where you and your child should feel comfortable enough to relax with the pressure firmly off.

If possible, create a separate play area for younger children, even if that consists of a box of their toys and a playmat in a corner of the living room.

Bring in personal touches to your home — frame family photos and hang them on the walls, collect artwork or display a few of your child's best creative efforts.

Discourage behaviour that makes your child feel unsafe — limit shouting and arguments.

KEEP ROUTINES

Children often fear the unknown and find change stressful and upsetting, which can lead to anger and mood changes. Encouraging your child to follow a routine from a young age helps them feel safe and also nurtures trust between you.

You might consider setting a routine for:

- **Getting ready in the morning**
- **Meal and snack times**
- **Bathtime and bedtime**
- **Chores, such as housework and cooking**
- **Family time and playtime**

But don't discourage spontaneity or the odd fun surprise either!

Bedtime routine

Try to establish a good bedtime routine fairly early in your child's life so that they grow accustomed to winding down at the end of the day and preparing for sleep.

A simple routine to follow is "bath, book and bed". You can include additions, such as having a milky drink and supper or listening to soothing music.

By setting a basic order and time frame, your child knows what to expect at the end of each day.

As they grow, they'll take ownership of their bedtime rituals. However, by laying the ground rules for a calming evening routine, you'll teach them an invaluable life skill.

Morning routine

Mornings can be stressful! Try to stick to a calm and ordered routine.

Prepare the night before by having school clothes and shoes ready and the table set for breakfast. Store coats, school bags and sports kits in the same place — a hook or cupboard — where you can easily grab them.

Rise earlier than your kids so you've had time to wash and dress before they get up. Set down ground rules — do your kids need to be dressed in their clothes for the day before they have breakfast or afterwards?

Make sure they've brushed their teeth — overseen by you, if necessary. Don't forget hair brushing, too.

Ask everyone to be ready at least five minutes before you're due to leave — that way, there's time to solve last-minute problems.

HOUSE RULES

Set some house rules for your family. These don't have to be strict or unbending but should represent your family values.

First, discuss these with your partner, if you have one. Once you have a clear idea of what you'd like to achieve, explain the rules to your children. Once everyone is in agreement, make it official.

Write down your rules and display them somewhere everyone can read them.

House rules may include:

- **Clear away your toys when you've finished playing.**
- **Don't talk over anyone.**
- **Treat each other — and their property — with respect.**
- **Be polite.**

Teaching self-care

Learning the art of self-care can boost your child's self-esteem, leaving them less at risk of depression and anxiety.

Bath or shower your child from a young age, teaching them to clean themselves. Brush your child's teeth twice a day and encourage them to do it themselves once they're old enough.

Brush your child's hair and show them how to put dirty clothes in the laundry basket and to select clean clothes to wear.

Teach your child that self-care isn't just about maintaining physical health and appearance but is equally about resting and nurturing their mind and sense of well-being.

The Children's Society offers useful pointers for children and self-care on their website.

Downtime

Children need regular breaks from timetables to amuse themselves with the pressure firmly off. Overscheduling your child with extracurricular activities and social engagements can lead to them feeling overwhelmed. For many children, feeling stressed and stifled by external expectations can trigger angry outbursts.

So consider cutting down on your child's out-of-school classes and give them opportunities for unstructured activity. This may mean allowing them space and time to draw, read, listen to music, build junk models, play with toys or spend time outdoors. Try not to rely on screens for downtime.

Healthy gut for a healthy mind

It sounds bizarre but scientists have found a strong link between gut health and mental health. In fact, some experts describe our stomachs as our "second brain", which can influence moods and well-being. Those with unhealthy guts have been found more likely to suffer from depression. That's because gut microbes produce and regulate "happy hormones", including serotonin and dopamine.

You can keep your child's gut healthy by ensuring they:

- **Eat three regular meals a day and avoid unhealthy snacks**
- **Cut down on sugar**
- **Avoid highly processed foods**
- **Eat more fibre**
- **Consume more plant-based foods**
- **Cut down on meat**
- **Eat oily fish**
- **Consume extra-virgin olive oil instead of other oils and fats**
- **Eat probiotic foods, such as live yoghurts, to encourage gut microbes to grow**

CHAPTER 6

Life Skills

By teaching your child how to navigate tricky situations, such as conflict with friends or overcoming self-doubt, you'll boost their sense of self-esteem and self-trust and also build their resilience. By instilling these values in your child early on, you'll help them learn to cope with difficult emotions as they grow up, as this chapter outlines.

Teach conflict resolution

Give your child pointers for dealing with disagreements with siblings and friends.

Outline the scenario to them to show that you understand and to help them identify their feelings: "You're sad because Sarah said she doesn't want to go to the park with you. Is that right?"

Teach them about "I" statements. Ask them to replace "Sarah won't go to the park with me and now I don't like her" with "It made me sad when Sarah didn't want to go to the park." This helps explain their viewpoint to the other child.

Encourage them to listen to the other child's "I" statement because teamwork is the fairest solution to conflict.

Let them know that it's fine – and sometimes advisable – to walk away and find an adult to help if they can't reach a solution among themselves.

Express big emotions safely

Teach your child that it's okay to have strong feelings and that everyone experiences them at some time.

But encourage them to express themselves in a way that won't put anyone at risk. Be firm when you explain to them that hitting, punching, scratching, biting and throwing things is not acceptable.

Instead, suggest that your child explores other ways of expressing big emotions. They could:

- Talk about how they feel

- Go for a run or kick a ball about (being active is a great way to channel anger and frustration as well as burning off excess energy and adrenalin)

- Get creative by writing, drawing or painting their feelings, or even writing a song or piece of music about their emotions

TEACH BOUNDARIES

Challenging boundaries is all part of a child's development but, as a parent, you must set behavioural limits and teach them healthy boundaries.

Sticking to a regular routine helps them learn basic boundaries, such as when they should go to bed or eat. (See Chapter 5 for more tips on routines.) Your child should also learn physical parameters including respecting people's personal space and not taking things belonging to others.

It's important that they also learn about emotional bounds; that their feelings and needs are separate to those of other people. This guides them not to unfairly blame others for their own emotions. Additionally, it protects them from wrongly taking responsibility for other people's feelings, which can be damaging and stressful.

School issues

Clues that your child is having school-related problems include complaining of headaches or stomach-aches on school days. They may lose their motivation or confide that they don't like school but may not be able to verbalize exactly why. It could be any number of reasons, such as:

- **Struggling with school work**
- **Clashing with a teacher**
- **Friendship problems**
- **Being bullied or bullying another child**
- **Getting distracted at school by problems at home**
- **More complex, undiagnosed issues, such as ADHD, dyslexia or autism**

If you discover that your child is being bullied – or that they are bullying another child – you should contact the school for support. The Anti-Bullying Alliance and YoungMinds organization offer guidance.

If you're concerned about them struggling with schoolwork or friendships or that they may have an undiagnosed issue such as dyslexia, you could contact a trusted teacher at your child's school. For concerns over clashes with a particular teacher, it is best to contact the school's leadership team.

Friendship problems

Although it's hard watching your child struggling with friendship problems, try to remember that it's normal. Learning to navigate conflict is an important life skill and part of growing up. Listen to your child rather than immediately rushing to "fix" things. Empathize; don't belittle or minimize their problems. This will reassure them that you're supportive.

Ask questions to help them articulate their emotions, such as: "How did it feel when Tom said that to you?"

Encourage them to come up with problem-solving ideas and tell them about your own experiences of friendship issues.

Make it clear that any form of bullying is unacceptable, whether they're on the receiving end or they are instigating it.

COPING WITH ANGRY THOUGHTS

If your child is struggling with angry thoughts about themselves, other people or a situation out of their control, gently persuade them to confide in you.

If they're struggling to vocalize their feelings, encourage them to use their "anger thermometer" (see page 30) or to draw their anger or write it down.

Empathize with them and reassure them that angry thoughts are normal and will pass.

Encourage them to use mindfulness techniques to deflect angry thoughts such as breathing techniques or grounding exercises (see Chapter 3), or to engage in a physical activity, such as going for a walk or run.

Remind your child that thoughts aren't reality and that they shouldn't feel guilty for feeling angry. What counts is how they deal with these thoughts.

Teach them to ignore self-sabotaging thoughts

If your child is overwhelmed by their "inner critic" – the voice telling them that they're not as clever, funny or attractive as their peers – reassure them that most people struggle with insecurity at times.

If your child blurts out "I'm so stupid!" don't rush in with over-the-top positivity. Instead, help them "name" their feelings by asking: "You sound cross; why is that?"

Guide them to identify the issue – it could be a tricky maths question or perhaps they're unhappy with their drawing – and offer support.

Boost their self-esteem with encouragement and praise and point out their individual skills and talents. Teach them to embrace imperfection, too. (See page 61 for advice on perfectionism).

Dealing with negative opinions of others

Encourage your child to treat others with empathy, not negativity. For instance, if your child says, "Holly is so grumpy," explain that her friend may be struggling with her own emotions.

If your child consistently describes peers as "aggressive" or "mean", it's possible that they may be prone to "hostile attribution bias". This term is used by professionals after research* found that some people repeatedly blame peer issues on perceived deliberate actions by others — and that children who believe others are always trying to upset them are more likely to react angrily.

If this seems familiar to you, perhaps try explaining to your child that they're misreading social situations. However, kids particularly struggling may need guidance from a professional to help them see how perceived problems with peers are often accidental — and to learn how to brush these off and move on. (For advice on seeking help, see Chapter 8.)

*Source: First study by William Nasby, Ken Dodge and Nicki Crick in 1980

SELF-SOOTHING SKILLS

Equip your child with the skills to calm themselves in stressful situations. To enable your child to take a moment away from whatever is upsetting them, advise them to try these simple activities:

- **Use positive self-encouragement, such as: "I can get through this; I am strong enough to cope".**

- **Practise breathing techniques (see page 51).**

- **Use a stress squeezer – your child could carry one in their pocket or bag.**

- **Run cool water over your hands if you can get to a basin.**

- **Go for a walk.**

- **Sit and write down their feelings.**

- **Have a drink of water.**

Answering difficult questions

Be prepared for your child to ask tricky questions and give yourself time to formulate an appropriate answer.

For instance, your child might suddenly ask whether their grandparents or another loved one is going to die – something you hadn't been expecting to broach just yet.

Try saying: "That's an important question and I'm going to have a think before I answer."

If your child is comparing your parenting style to that of their friends' parents, don't feel compelled to justify yourself. It's fine to reply: "Every family is different."

Experts suggest children under seven should be shielded from TV news. If your child is fearful of high-profile tragedies they've heard about, don't lie to them. However, it's advisable to limit information you give so that it's easier for them to comprehend.

Being interested

Pay attention to your child's interests. Research* has shown that children who have adults around them encouraging and nurturing their "sparks" or passions are generally healthier and more satisfied, along with having better friendships and greater empathy skills.

So when your child talks to you about things that excite them, listen. If they're not particularly vocal, notice activities they favour.

Be careful not to force your own interests or expectations on them. For example, you may hope your child will focus on athletics but if they'd rather take dance lessons, accept and respect that.

*Source: Search Institute

KNOWING WHEN TO REST

Sleep is necessary for physical and mental growth. Although every child has individual requirements, the average five-year-old needs 11 hours whereas a 15-year-old needs around nine hours, according to NHS guidelines. So it's important that your child knows how to wind down each evening. (See Chapter 5 for advice on bedtime routine.)

Tiredness often triggers mood changes so help your child to recognize when they need a rest from play or homework. A good way to encourage daytime rest is to steer your child to a quiet corner with a book or simple toy – a den is ideal for this. (See page 53 for tips on den-building.)

Give them a bit of responsibility

Delegating some age-appropriate tasks to your child is great for bolstering their self-esteem.

Start simply with something relatively straightforward and don't overload them. Rather than a vague "Tidy your room," give clear instructions, such as: "Please hang up all your clothes in your wardrobe."

Show your child how to do things correctly before asking them to fulfil their task by themselves.

Praise them when they've completed their task and teach them that if they help out, they'll have more time for fun. For example, you could say: "Once you've helped me water the plants, I'll play in the garden with you."

Learning resilience

Work on developing your child's resilience – an invaluable life skill that can help them cope with all manner of stressful situations.

- Spend lots of one-on-one time together to boost their sense of security and self-esteem.

- Help them identify difficult emotions, such as fear, anger, jealousy and sadness, and explain that they're normal and will pass.

- Don't immediately jump in to solve your child's problems – give them time to work things out themselves.

- Let them take healthy risks – it's how they'll learn to trust their judgement.

- Teach them that a certain degree of "failure" and "mistakes" are part of life's learning journey and that you'll support them through these.

- Help them accept that they'll experience discomfort and disappointment sometimes, but that these difficult situations won't last forever.

CULTIVATE SELF-TRUST

Balance your desire to protect your child with the need to teach them to trust their own instincts and abilities.

- **Ask them such questions as "How did that make you feel?" to encourage them to explore their emotions.**

- **Teach them about their instincts, why we have them and why it's important to listen to them — such as not feeling comfortable in certain situations.**

- **Value their choices and don't belittle their worries.**

- **Praise and encourage them when they try new things but reassure them that you'll support them however it turns out.**

- **Don't smother them; teach them to face challenges head-on.**

CHAPTER 7

Looking to Yourself

When you're focused on parenting, your own
needs may take a back seat. However, it's important
to be a role model for your child by taking care
of yourself and keeping a check on your own
moods and behaviour. This chapter offers advice
on looking to yourself in order to help your child.

Identify how you express anger

Have a think about the way you react to angry feelings. Do you shout or sulk? Do you lash out with words or show your anger physically? Perhaps you don't vocalize your feelings at all but turn angry thoughts in on yourself.

Everyone deals with anger in their own way but you may notice that your own moods follow a recognizable pattern.

Keep a note of your feelings and reactions to difficult situations so that you can build a picture of your general behaviour. You may already be aware of the way you react to certain situations or you may surprise yourself once it's written down clearly.

Look for your stress points

Do you find mornings stressful, as you try to organize your child and get them out of the house? Or is bedtime a flashpoint for you? Perhaps you find mealtimes hard work? Maybe you find your own moods triggered by your child's angry outbursts — especially when they're directed at you. There's a good chance that you find yourself more likely to lose your cool when you're tired, emotional or worried. By pinpointing stress points in your routine, you can start thinking about how to tackle these situations more calmly and being a good role model for your child.

LEAD BY EXAMPLE

Aim to be a positive role model for your child – someone they watch for guidance on how to react to situations.

Research* suggests that personality traits are more strongly defined by genetics than circumstance. However, remember that behavioural patterns can be learned – and your child is learning from you.

Experiment with self-soothing exercises discussed in this book and tell your child how you're dealing with your feelings. For example: "I'm so cross about dropping all those eggs on the floor but I'm going to count to ten and remind myself that it was just an accident and then I'll feel better."

* Source: Minnesota Study of Twins Reared Apart from 1979 to 1999

Self-care for you

As well as teaching your child the value of self-care, make sure you're looking after yourself, too, both physically and mentally. Self-care doesn't have to be complicated or expensive; it can be as simple as running yourself a relaxing bath after a long day.

Other ways to look after yourself include:

- **Eating a healthy, balanced diet**
- **Getting enough sleep**
- **Exercising regularly**
- **Getting outside in the fresh air**
- **Visiting somewhere different for a change of scene**
- **Seeing friends**
- **Spending time alone**
- **Learning to say no to others to avoid feeling overwhelmed**
- **Scheduling time for self-care, whether it's sparing half an hour to read a book or booking in a trip to the hairdresser**

Be kind to yourself

Treat yourself as you'd ideally treat others — with kindness.

Self-compassion means being understanding towards yourself. Rather than listening to your "inner critic" (see Chapter 6 for advice on self-sabotaging thoughts), talk to yourself as forgivingly as you would to a friend.

For example, don't berate yourself for forgetting to pick up more milk. Instead, cut yourself some slack by telling yourself: "I'm really busy and preoccupied with work and I'm only human, after all. We have enough milk to last until tomorrow."

Research* has found that self-compassion correlates with higher life satisfaction, wisdom, optimism, happiness and emotional intelligence. It also lowers the risk of depression and anxiety.

*Source: Kristin Neff, 2009

RETHINKING YOUR CHILD'S STRONG EMOTIONS

Learn how to reframe your child's moods and behaviour by focusing on the positive, not the negative.

For example, instead of seeing your child as too opinionated and loud, remind yourself of their good qualities and try reframing their personality as confident and assertive.

Rather than feeling weary at their emotional outbursts, remind yourself that it's positive that they are able to express themselves and feel safe with you, as a parent, to behave in this way.

View their behaviour with empathy. Your child doesn't yet have the maturity or life experience to know the answers for managing their moods. It's your role to help them learn.

Practise self-acceptance

Just as you should encourage your child to ignore their "inner critic" and accept themselves as they are, you should do the same.

Self-acceptance means recognizing your strengths and weaknesses, being realistic about your capabilities and being happy with yourself, despite your flaws.

Benefits of self-acceptance include mood regulation and positive emotions, a greater sense of self-worth and less chance of depression.

Be honest with your child about yourself. For example, you could say: "I'm not the greatest cook but I've always been good at gardening." This shows your child that it's healthy to accept your own weaknesses and recognize your strengths, rather than aiming for perfection or trying to be someone else – and will encourage them to do the same.

Make time for yourself

Carve out some "me time" away from parenting duties and your other responsibilities – it's a great morale booster. It can be tricky to make time for yourself when you have a child, but it's important not to lose track of who you are as a person or ignore your own needs.

Make a list – mental or otherwise – of things you'd like to do for yourself. Work out when you can start fulfilling these things – perhaps when your child is at school or is being looked after by their other parent or relative.

Make a note on your calendar so that no one forgets and stick to it! Don't feel guilty either – you've earned this!

CREATE A MENTAL HEALTH SHELF

Find an easy-to-reach home for your most treasured, precious items – cosy blanket, inspiring books, feel-good movies, special photos and stress squeezers.

Make one for your child, too, and encourage them to personalize it with familiar, reassuring posessions.

If you don't have a spare shelf, you could use a box, basket or drawer – it doesn't matter as long as your special things are easy to access in tricky times when you're in need of comfort.

CHAPTER 8

Seek Support

There is no shame in asking for help;
on the contrary, it shows incredible strength.
Try confiding in trusted friends and family
for emotional support and, if you feel it
would help, talk to a professional or a
specific organization for guidance on your
options and the next available steps.

When to ask for help

You may be concerned that you're not making much progress with your child's moods, or that their mood has been low for a considerable time. You might be worried that their anger could harm them or those around them.

In these instances, you could consider talking to a trusted professional such as:

- **Your child's teacher**
- **The school nurse**
- **The school special educational needs coordinator (SENCo)**
- **Your family doctor or nurse**

If necessary, you may be referred to a local children's mental health service, specialist children's counsellor or therapist. You can also refer your child to a specialist without having seen your family doctor.

You may want to have your child assessed for such conditions as autism, ADHD or sensory processing disorder, which can have an impact on a child's moods.

Self-help books and podcasts

Expand your knowledge by reading self-help books. There is a wealth of books available covering parenting and child behavioural issues.

If you struggle to find time for reading, audio books are a great alternative and can be downloaded online.

You could also consider listening to some podcasts by experts or other parents.

Download the audio book to your phone or click on the podcast and listen while you're getting on with other things.

Here are some useful podcasts to get you started:

- Peace Out – short stories to help kids relax.

- BBC *Woman's Hour* – this daily podcast regularly features experts discussing various parenting and mental-health issues.

- The Mind charity podcast – presented by Mind ambassador and Heart FM DJ Matt Wilkinson.

TALKING TO YOUR CHILD ABOUT PROFESSIONAL SUPPORT

If you're considering seeking professional support, be honest with your child.

Reassure them that they're not in trouble or at risk of being "punished". Make sure they know that you're not angry or disappointed in them, but that things can't carry on as they are. Be clear that your desire to find help comes from a place of love.

Make sure they know that you and the professionals they may see will be on their side at all times. You could say: "We want to help you understand your feelings, thoughts and behaviour."

Explain to your child that by seeking professional support, you're hoping they will eventually feel happier and find life easier.

Preparing to visit your doctor

Talk to your child about what to expect from their first appointment with a doctor. If they're prepared beforehand, they're less likely to feel anxious and more likely to cooperate.

Use age-appropriate terms and explain the situation calmly and simply. For example, you could say: "We're going to speak to the doctor about the way you feel and behave sometimes."

Reiterate that you and the professionals they may see will be on their side at all times. You could say: "We want to help you understand your emotions."

Making decisions

Be honest and clear when you explain options to your child. They must never feel unsafe or forced into anything.

Like adults, young people aged 16 or 17 can decide on their medical treatment, unless they don't have sufficient capacity. Children under 16 can consent if they understand what is involved.

Otherwise, an adult with parental responsibility can consent to a child's treatment but under the United Nations' Convention on the Rights of the Child, the child's opinion must be given serious consideration during decision making.

By reassuring your child that their wishes will be considered, you will reinforce the sense of trust between you, your child and the professionals helping them.

TAKING A HOLISTIC APPROACH

View your child as a person with many facets and take time to appreciate their attributes, whether these include kindness, sensitivity, persistence or something else. Tell your child that you value their talents and skills so that they don't fall into a trap of seeing themselves solely as a person with "anger issues".

Taking a holistic approach means looking at the bigger picture with regards to both your child's character and the situation you find yourselves in.

Try not to focus too much on their difficult behaviour, either privately or in conversation with them. Reassure them that their problems don't define them. Encourage your child to enjoy the simple things in life and celebrate joyful moments, however small.

Types of support available

There may be several options available to your child.

They could be referred for confidential counselling. They may be recommended for therapy, such as art or music therapy, either one-to-one or in a group setting.

Your child's school may offer additional guidance from teachers or external professionals, such as occupational therapists. If your child is assessed for such a condition as autism, they should receive support from relevant professionals during this process.

The international organization Ditch the Label tackles children's mental-health issues globally.

If you or your child is in crisis, seek urgent medical assistance. In the UK, you can contact the Samaritans, with other suicide-prevention charities available worldwide.

Reaching out to other parents

Don't be afraid to turn to other parents. You may find that they've experienced a similar situation.

They may have useful advice to offer and might give recommendations for experts or organizations that could help.

Even if other parents can't tell you exactly what to do, it can be comforting to hear from someone who's "been there".

Whether you feel comfortable confiding in relatives, friends or other parents you find through online or "real-life" support groups, you may well find truth in the old saying: "A problem shared is a problem halved."

LOOKING TO THE FUTURE

Stay hopeful and positive; try to look at the bigger picture if you are feeling overwhelmed by your child's moods.

Remind yourself that, as with many parenting issues, "This too will pass." Also, be comforted that, by picking up this book, you've already proved yourself a thoughtful parent who cares deeply about your child's well-being, now and in the future.

Be confident in your ability to work through this tricky time with your child.

Don't put pressure on yourself by setting deadlines. However, try to believe that one day – hopefully in the not-too-distant future – you and your child will both feel more settled and content.

Conclusion

Hopefully, you will have found this book both reassuring and inspiring. Refer back to it whenever you feel the need for extra guidance and information.

There is, of course, no easy solution or fail-safe method for helping your child manage their moods. However, by trying different techniques, along with offering unconditional love and support, stay positive that you can navigate tricky times together.

By teaching your child to cope with difficult emotions, rather than being overwhelmed by them, you will give them a wonderful gift – the ability and skills to grow into a happy, stable and contented adult.

Have you enjoyed this book?

If so, why not write a review on your favourite website? If you're interested in finding out more about our books, find us on Facebook at **Summersdale Publishers** and follow us on Twitter at **@Summersdale**.

Thanks very much for buying this Summersdale book.

www.summersdale.com